INCOME TAX COMPLIANCE BY U.S. CITIZENS AND U.S. LAWFUL PERMANENT RESIDENTS RESIDING OUTSIDE THE UNITED STATES AND RELATED ISSUES

Department of the Treasury
Office of Tax Policy

Fredonia Books
Amsterdam, The Netherlands

Income Tax Compliance by U.S. Citizens and U.S.
Lawful Permanent Residents Residing Outside the
United States and Related Issues

by
U.S. Department of the Treasury
Office of Tax Policy

ISBN: 1-4101-0815-5

Copyright © 2005 by Fredonia Books

Reprinted from the 1998 edition

Fredonia Books
Amsterdam, The Netherlands
http://www.fredoniabooks.com

INCOME TAX COMPLIANCE BY U.S. CITIZENS AND U.S. LAWFUL PERMANENT RESIDENTS RESIDING OUTSIDE THE UNITED STATES AND RELATED ISSUES

TABLE OF CONTENTS

EXECUTIVE SUMMARY

This report responds to section 513 of the Health Insurance Portability and Accountability Act, Pub. L. 104-191, which directs the Secretary of the Treasury to prepare a report that describes income tax compliance by U.S. citizens and lawful permanent residents residing outside the United States and that recommends measures to improve such compliance, including improved coordination between executive branch agencies. As suggested in the House Ways and Means Committee report accompanying the legislation, the report also reviews the process through which the Department of State determines when U.S. citizenship has been lost, and discusses possible changes to that process in light of its significance for tax purposes. *See* H.R. Rep. No. 104-736, at 329-330.

Part I of the report summarizes the current law regarding the taxation of U.S. citizens and lawful permanent residents living abroad and the income tax filing requirements placed on such persons. Part I also describes the tax regime that applies to former U.S. citizens and long-term permanent residents whose loss of such status had for one of its principal purposes the avoidance of U.S. taxes.

Part II details initiatives the Internal Revenue Service has undertaken to measure and improve compliance by U.S. taxpayers living overseas, including a discussion of Internal Revenue Service's successful Middle East Compliance Initiative and a discussion of a demographic study the Internal Revenue Service is currently conducting that will allow it to more effectively apply its enforcement resources. Part II also discusses factors currently limiting compliance enforcement.

Part III of the report discusses the extent to which the Department of State and the Immigration and Naturalization Service collect information that might aid the Internal Revenue Service in determining and improving compliance. The discussion suggests ways in which the Department of State and the Immigration and Naturalization Service could make the information currently collected more useful to the Internal Revenue Service, describes the information those agencies are not currently collecting that could aid the Internal Revenue Service in determining and improving compliance, and notes the changes to those agencies' information disclosure policies and information disclosure constraints that might be necessary for information that the agencies now collect to be made available to the Internal Revenue Service.

Part IV of the report describes the current law regarding the definition of "U.S. citizen" for income tax purposes and discusses possible changes to the definition that might allow the Internal Revenue Service to more effectively allocate its resources to identify certain non-complying U.S. taxpayers living overseas and to better prevent tax avoidance by U.S. citizens who expatriate to avoid U.S. taxes. The inclusion in the report of these possible changes (like the inclusion in Section I.C of possible changes to the expatriation taxation rules) is intended to serve as a basis for discussion, and not as a legislative recommendation.

Part V concludes that directed application of the Internal Revenue Service's proven compliance-improvement methods, such as were used in the Internal Revenue Service's successful Middle East Compliance Initiative, discussed in Section II.B, is the most cost-effective way to improve overseas compliance and concludes that the Internal Revenue Service should continue to pursue its demographic study, discussed in Section II.A, to provide that direction. It is therefore the recommendation of this report that the Internal Revenue Service draw upon its extensive compliance-improvement experience, combined with the results of its demographic study, to appropriately allocate its resources to projects and initiatives that properly balance the goals of efficient revenue collection with the legitimate privacy and other interests of Americans living and traveling overseas. Such projects and initiatives should include: analysis of local information sources, such as local financial news media, and Department of State and Department of Labor data, to identify employers of U.S. citizens, organizations with U.S. citizenship membership, education resources for U.S. citizens or dependents and any other data that would aid in targeting education and compliance projects; identification of local tax practitioners used by U.S. citizens to provide such practitioners with the resources and education necessary to improve compliance with U.S. tax laws; identification of local media outlets accessed by U.S. citizens and development of specialized media releases to educate U.S. citizens regarding identified areas of non-compliance; development and implementation of market segment education and compliance projects; conducting outreach and informational seminars; and pursuing appropriate individual examinations and investigations. *See* Section II.B. The Internal Revenue Service's demographic study, which should provide information that can help guide the application of these projects and initiatives, is scheduled for release in draft form later this summer.

I.   Summary of Current Law

A.   General Provisions

In general, U.S. citizens are required to file U.S. tax returns and to pay taxes on their worldwide taxable income, regardless of whether they reside inside or outside the United States. The United States also imposes a special tax regime on former citizens (and former long-term lawful permanent residents) whose loss of such status had for one of its principal purposes the avoidance of U.S. taxes.[1] *See* Section I.C, *infra*. The determination of who is a citizen for tax purposes, and when such citizenship is lost, is governed by the Immigration and Nationality Act ("INA"). *See* Treas. Reg. § 1.1-1(c) (referencing INA, 8 U.S.C. § 1401 *et seq.*); *see also* Section IV.A, *infra*.

A non-U.S. citizen generally is taxed in the same manner as a U.S. citizen, and is subject to the same filing requirements, if the individual is a "resident alien," as that term is defined in section 7701(b) of the Internal Revenue Code of 1986 (the "Code"). The term includes a person who is a lawful permanent resident of the United States (sometimes referred to as a "green card holder") at any time during the calendar year. Code § 7701(b)(1)(A)(i); *see also* Treas. Reg. § 301.7701(b)-1.

A citizen or resident alien need not file a tax return unless his or her gross income equals or exceeds certain minimum amounts.[2] Code § 6012(a). Even if a citizen or resident alien is required to file a return, two provisions of the Code -- the foreign earned income exclusion (and housing expense exclusion and deduction) and the foreign tax credit -- allow many U.S. citizens or resident aliens who reside abroad to reduce or eliminate their U.S. tax liability.

---

[1]In addition, the Immigration and Nationality Act ("INA") provides that the Immigration and Naturalization Service ("INS") may deny entry to the United States to any former U.S. citizen who officially renounces U.S. citizenship and who the Attorney General determines renounced citizenship for the purpose of avoiding U.S. taxation. INA § 212(a)(10)(E), 8 U.S.C. § 1182(a)(10)(E).

[2]For 1997, the threshold amounts were $6,800 for a single individual under the age of 65 and $12,200 for a married couple filing jointly both of whom are under the age of 65.

B. Foreign Earned Income Exclusion and Foreign Tax Credit (Code Sections 911 and 901)

The foreign earned income exclusion, pursuant to section 911 of the Code and regulations thereunder, allows a qualifying U.S. citizen or resident to exclude from gross income up to $72,000 of his or her foreign earned income.[3] In addition, the individual may exclude certain foreign housing costs paid on behalf of, or deduct certain foreign housing costs paid by, the individual that are in excess of a base amount.[4] To qualify for the exclusions or deduction, the individual must meet certain foreign residency tests. In addition, the individual generally must affirmatively elect to obtain the benefits of each such exclusion on IRS Form 2555 or on a comparable form attached to his or her timely filed tax return.[5] An election once made remains in effect unless revoked. As discussed in Section II.B, *infra*, the Internal Revenue Service ("IRS") has taken steps to educate U.S. citizens residing and working abroad of their obligation to file U.S. tax returns while overseas even if they earn less than the excludable amount. IRS has also taken steps to ease significantly the filing burden

---

[3]Section 911 was amended by section 1172 of the Taxpayer Relief Act of 1997, Pub. L. 105-34, to provide that the excludable amount would increase from $70,000 to $72,000 for calendar year 1998 and will increase an additional $2,000 a year for each year following until the year 2002, at which time the excludable amount will equal $80,000. That amount will be adjusted with respect to calendar year 2008 and thereafter for inflation occurring after calendar year 2006.

[4]The base amount is $9,426 for 1997.

[5]However, a taxpayer who does not timely file but who would owe no federal income tax after taking into account the section 911 exclusions may nevertheless elect the exclusions, and thus owe no U.S. federal income tax, on a Form 2555 attached to a late-filed Form 1040, even if the taxpayer does not file until after the Internal Revenue Service ("IRS") discovers and informs the taxpayer that the taxpayer has not filed a return. A taxpayer who would owe any federal income tax even taking into account the exclusions may elect the exclusions on a Form 2555 attached to a filed Form 1040 only if he files before he is discovered by the IRS not to have filed. *See* Treas. Reg. § 1.911-7(a)(2)(i)(D). The taxpayer who would owe any federal income tax may also be subject to penalties for the failure to timely file and pay. *See* Code § 6651.

for those U.S. citizens living and working overseas wishing to elect the exclusions who make less than the amount excludable under section 911, through the development and promotion of Form 2555EZ, discussed in Section II.B, *infra*.

The foreign tax credit under section 901 of the Code generally allows a person who pays income tax to a foreign government on foreign source income to claim a credit against U.S. income tax on that income, subject to certain limitations. This credit can be claimed by U.S. citizens and residents residing in the United States or abroad. In order to claim the credit, an individual must file IRS Form 1116 with his or her tax return.[6]

Nearly 50% of the returns filed by overseas citizens or resident aliens report no tax liability, primarily as a result of sections 911 and 901 of the Code. In addition, even among those overseas citizens or resident aliens who have been found by IRS not to have filed returns, the provisions of sections 911 and 901 still may operate to eliminate or reduce significantly the amount of U.S. tax owed.[7] For example, in one IRS compliance initiative, which the Government Accounting Office (the "GAO") studied in a 1993 report, *Tax Administration: IRS Activities to Increase Compliance of Overseas Taxpayers* (the "1993 GAO Report"), out of 176 overseas taxpayers that IRS contacted who hadn't filed returns, only one owed U.S. taxes, totaling $9,595. Similarly, in another initiative,

---

[6]The foreign tax credit provisions of the Code were simplified by the Taxpayer Relief Act of 1997, Pub. L. 105-34. Among other changes, an individual with no more than $300 ($600 in the case of married persons filing jointly) of creditable foreign taxes and no foreign source income other than passive income will be exempt from the foreign tax credit limitation rules for taxable years beginning after December 31, 1997. In addition, such an individual will not be required to file Form 1116 in order to obtain the benefit of the foreign tax credit.

[7]The Government Accounting Office ("GAO") noted the effect of the provisions in a 1993 report, *Tax Administration: IRS Activities to Increase Compliance of Overseas Taxpayers* (the "1993 GAO Report").

only $2,126 was owed from a group of 140 delinquent filers, and in a third only $5,345 was owed

from a group of 62 overseas nonfilers. *See* 1993 GAO Report, at 9-10.[8] Although these samples are

clearly too small for any definitive general conclusions to be drawn from them, Treasury believes the

samples do indicate that with respect to U.S. taxpayers working overseas, a taxpayer's failure to file

a U.S. tax return does not necessarily indicate that the taxpayer is not paying the taxes he or she owes

to the United States. Therefore an initiative aimed merely at increasing overseas filing compliance

may not necessarily raise sufficient revenue to justify the cost of such an initiative.

C.   Expatriation to Avoid Tax (Code Section 877)

The Health Insurance Portability and Accountability Act of 1996, Pub. L. 104-191 (the "Act")

significantly modified sections 877, 2107, and 2501 of the Code. These sections of the Code, as

amended, impose a special tax regime on former citizens and former long-term lawful permanent

residents whose loss of such status had for one of its principal purposes the avoidance of U.S. taxes.[9]

In general, section 877 subjects certain former U.S. citizens who have relinquished their U.S.

citizenship, and certain former long-term residents who have relinquished their status as long-term

residents (*e.g.*, former long-term green card holders who have surrendered their green cards), to U.S.

tax on certain income having a U.S. nexus, for the ten-year period following the relinquishment. A

tax under section 877 is imposed on all who expatriate unless the expatriation "did not have for one

---

[8]The 1993 GAO Report stated, however, that the data was too limited to be able to predict the potential revenue impact of undertaking additional enforcement actions against overseas taxpayers. *See* 1993 GAO Report, p. 9.

[9]The Immigration and Nationality Act was also amended in 1996 and now provides, as was noted in Section I.A, *supra*, that INS may deny entry to any former U.S. citizen determined by the Attorney General to have renounced U.S. citizenship for the purpose of avoiding U.S. tax.

of its principal purposes the avoidance of [U.S. income or estate and gift] taxes". Any individual with a net worth of $500,000 or more (adjusted for inflation) on the date of expatriation or who has an average annual net income tax liability for the five years preceding expatriation of $100,000 or more (adjusted for inflation) is irrebuttably presumed to have expatriated for tax-motivated reasons (except as discussed below), and thereby is subject to tax under section 877 regardless of actual intent. All expatriates are required under the Code to provide upon expatriation a statement indicating residence and citizenship. In the case of expatriates with gross assets having an aggregate fair market value in excess of $500,000, a detailed statement of assets and liabilities is also required. *See* Notice 97-19, 1997-10 I.R.B. 40, section IX; *see also* Code § 6039G(a), (b).

Section 877 in general requires that IRS determine the intent of the expatriate in expatriating. In recognition of the difficulty of determining subjective intent, section 877 was amended by the Act to provide objective criteria pursuant to which certain taxpayers are irrebuttably presumed to have expatriated to avoid U.S. taxes. Such taxpayers are thereby subject to tax under section 877 regardless of their actual intent in expatriating.

Section 877 also provides, however, that certain expatriates who would otherwise be subject to the irrebuttable presumption can avoid the presumption by submitting a ruling request for a determination as to whether such loss had for one of its principal purposes the avoidance of U.S. taxes. The section provides that only a limited class of expatriates are eligible to submit a ruling request and thereby avoid the presumption. That class consists of:

(i) expatriates who were dual citizens at birth who have remained citizens of the second country;

(ii) expatriates who at the time of expatriation (or within a reasonable period thereafter) were

5

(or became) citizens of their country of birth or the country of birth of their spouses or of either of their (the expatriates') parents;

(iii) expatriates who for the 10 years prior to expatriation were present in the United States for no more than 30 days in any year; and

(iv) expatriates who renounced U.S. citizenship before attaining the age of 18½.[10]

IRS' Office of Assistant Commissioner (International) ("ACI") has primary jurisdiction for overseas taxpayers and is thus charged with the enforcement of section 877. Although the Act's addition to Code section 877 of the irrebuttable presumption does aid in enforcement efforts, ACI will likely still face severe enforcement difficulties. With respect to taxpayers to whom the irrebuttable presumption does not apply, it is very difficult to demonstrate the required intent. With respect to expatriates to whom the presumption does apply, and who thereby are subject to tax under section 877 regardless of actual intent, tracking down and auditing such taxpayers will often be difficult. Moreover, even when such persons are audited, they may in fact owe little or no tax, if, for example, the section 877 tax is avoided through advance planning that minimizes the recognition of U.S.-nexus income during the ten-year period. Further, even if the expatriate does in fact owe tax, the expatriate may have no assets the IRS can reach, particularly if many years have passed since the expatriation, and would therefore effectively be immune to IRS collection efforts.

Alternatives to the current expatriation taxation regime may address the administrative and substantive problems inherent in Code section 877 as revised by the Act. For example, an expatriation tax placed on the unrealized appreciation in the expatriate's assets at the time of expatriation (that is, a regime like the one generally applicable to corporate "expatriations" under

---

[10]The statute also allows for additional categories to be created by regulation.

section 367(a) of the Code) may be easier for IRS to administer, as it would not require that IRS track the individual for the 10 years following expatriation, as is currently the case. The tax would be assessed in the year of expatriation and would be imposed with respect to gain inherent in assets at that time, as opposed to income realized up to 10 years later, and therefore the assessment, collection and enforcement problems inherent Code section 877 as revised by the Act would be somewhat ameliorated (although it should be noted that, even under this regime, a taxpayer planning to expatriate could try to move his or her assets beyond IRS' reach before expatriating, thereby hindering collection). In addition to these salutary administrative effects, this approach would implement the policy that it is appropriate to tax, at the time a person expatriates, the gains that have accrued while the person was a citizen or long-term resident of the United States.

Other alternatives should also be considered, including the regime put forward by Senator Moynihan and Representative Gibbons in 1995, which, very generally, would impose a tax upon expatriation on any gain inherent in any asset held by an expatriate, but would allow the expatriate to elect instead to be subject to continued U.S. taxation, including estate and gift taxation, with respect to any asset. *See* Joint Committee on Taxation, *Issues Presented by Proposals to Modify the Tax Treatment of Expatriation*, JCS-17-95, at 42-45 (the "JCT Report").

II.   Compliance Measurement and Improvement

A.   Demographic Study of Overseas Compliance

The Internal Revenue Service is currently conducting a demographic study of U.S. citizens living in certain overseas geographic areas to measure more accurately current tax compliance by U.S. citizens living abroad. This study, which is scheduled to be released in draft form later this summer, is based on foreign countries' census data, on United States return filing data, and on other data, such as data regarding U.S. Social Security Administration payments and U.S. Civil Service retirement payments. The study will provide estimates of the number of American citizens living in each country profiled as well as aggregate per-country information regarding types of employment, income levels, and other demographic information with respect to those American citizens. Based on the information provided to IRS, the study will yield, for each country profiled, on an aggregated basis, estimated rates of filing and payment compliance by American citizens living in that country. IRS estimates that approximately 80% of the American citizens living overseas live in the countries to be profiled in the study.

With information the study will provide regarding current aggregate compliance levels in profiled countries, IRS will develop and implement more targeted, and thus more effective, compliance strategies. It is anticipated the compliance initiatives will employ methods used in IRS' successful Middle East Compliance Initiative, discussed in Section II.B, *infra*.

B.   Efforts to Improve Compliance

IRS has undertaken and is continuing to undertake numerous measures to improve voluntary compliance by taxpayers overseas. Based on IRS' experience in tax administration and based on its standard enforcement techniques, IRS has developed overseas compliance initiatives that focus on three general areas:

- Reducing taxpayer burden;

- Increasing taxpayer education; and

- Improving IRS' enforcement results.

8

Recent IRS overseas compliance initiatives include the following:

(i)   Completion of the Middle East Compliance Initiative, focusing on increased taxpayer education and IRS enforcement efforts. This program focused on persons who moved to Kuwait following the 1991 Gulf War as a result of the extensive reconstruction needed in the area and is believed to be responsible in part for a 51% increase in the number of returns filed by U.S. citizens residing in the region;[11]

(ii)   Development of a simplified form for overseas taxpayers to elect the foreign earned income exclusion under Code section 911, discussed in Section I.B, *supra*. IRS' goal in developing this Form 2555EZ was to make return filing it easier for those individuals who are least likely to owe any U.S. taxes, *i.e.*, persons who make less than the amount excludable under section 911. The following table shows the response to this simplified form during its first three years in use:

Tax Year	Form 2555	Form 2555EZ	Total	% Increase in Total	EZ % of Total
1989	194,017	-	194,017	-	-
1990	204,053	-	204,053	5.17%	-
1991	222,057	-	222,057	8.82%	-
1992	209,629	43,000	252,629	13.76%	17.02%
1993	192,924	51,004	243,928	-3.44%	20.91%
1994	207,289	49,951	257,240	5.46%	19.42%

[Sources: IRS Publication 1304, *Individual Income Tax Returns Statistics of Income*, Table 1.4 (1989 - 1994); AC(I) Information Systems Division]

As the above statistics indicate, total filings jumped in 1992, the year the Form 2555EZ was introduced, and Forms 2555EZ are now a significant percentage of the total forms filed. At the time this report was drafted, final numbers for 1995 and 1996 were not yet available but preliminary numbers indicate that total filings will increase again, by approximately 3% for each year. IRS intends to continue to promote Form 2555EZ through its taxpayer education efforts and by including it in

---

[11]Other factors also contributed to the increase in filings, such as the increase in the number of U.S. taxpayers in the region after the Gulf War, although such factors alone do not account for the magnitude of the increase.

the individual tax package mailing;

(iii)   Revision of Publication 593, *Tax Highlights for U.S. Citizens and Residents Going Abroad*, to encourage eligible taxpayers to file Form 2555EZ;

(iv)   Development and implementation of a program to provide tax assistance to members of the U.S. military serving in Operation Joint Endeavor, supporting the no-fly zone in Iraq, and to those serving in other military operations abroad;

(v)   Revision of Publication 519, *U.S. Tax Guide for Aliens*, and the instructions to the 1996 Form 1040NR, *U.S. Nonresident Alien Income Tax Return*, to make former citizens and long-term resident aliens aware of their potential tax liability under section 877 as revised by the Act;

(vi)   Improvement of access to tax forms overseas through various initiatives, including the improvement of IRS' forms distribution process and IRS' automated system for recording and updating addresses. In addition, IRS will continue to post forms, instructions and publications on IRS' World Wide Web page on the Internet (at www.irs.ustreas.gov/prod/forms_pubs) so that U.S. taxpayers overseas will be able to access, download and print the necessary U.S. tax forms and the necessary guidance to complete and file required U.S. tax returns correctly;

(vii)   Addition of a statement to all U.S. passports issued after early 1993 reminding the holder that all U.S. citizens working and residing overseas are required to file U.S. tax returns and report based on their worldwide income;

(viii)   Completion and continuation of numerous market segment compliance projects targeted at areas of suspected noncompliance, which have to date yielded on average over $4,000 additional tax due per taxpayer and which have the general effect of deterring others from risking non-compliance, including such projects as the:

☐ Airline Pilot Initiative, designed to enhance compliance by U.S. persons piloting for U.S. or foreign airlines and any person piloting for U.S. airlines;

☐ Highly Compensated Executives Initiative, focusing on individuals who improperly claim tax benefits for contributions to certain foreign pension plans;

☐ U.S. Agency for International Development Initiative, ensuring that the agency's field missions are correctly treating workers as employees for tax purposes;

☐ Educator & Scholar Initiative, designed to enhance compliance among the scholar/educator segment of overseas Americans;

☐ 30/30 Worker Initiative, targeting individuals who are not eligible for a claimed section 911 foreign earned income exclusion because they do not meet the definition of "qualified individual" (*e.g.*, workers who every 60 days spend 30 days working on an offshore oil platform in foreign territorial waters and 30 days on leave in the United States);

☐ Schedule C Filer Initiative, identifying individuals engaged in a trade or business in which both personal services and capital are material income-producing factors and whose reported earned income exceeds the 30-percent-of-net-profits limitation of section 911(d)(2)(B), *see also* Treas. Reg. § 1.911-3(b)(2), and who thus may have claimed a foreign earned income exclusion greater than permitted; and

☐ Foreign Partnership Initiative, examining Forms 1040 and 1040NR that improperly classify certain income from foreign partnerships as passive, rather than active, income for purposes of the passive activity loss provisions.

Because of its limited compliance resources, IRS intends to focus its future compliance efforts on those areas of noncompliance that have the greatest potential for increased tax collection. As noted in Section I.B, *supra*, simply improving overseas tax return filing compliance will not necessarily result in a commensurate increase in tax revenues, because of the foreign tax credit of Code section 901 and the foreign earned income exclusion (and housing expense exclusion and deduction) of Code section 911.

Accordingly, IRS is developing new programs, principally the demographic study described in Section II.A, *supra*, to identify those overseas taxpayers who do not file returns and who are most likely to actually owe U.S. tax. Once IRS has completed the demographic study, IRS will use the study to identify those countries with the highest non-compliance levels with respect to filing and the highest levels of non-compliance with respect to payment of taxes owed. With respect to those countries, the IRS will then:

- scan local information sources, such as local financial news media, and Department of State and Department of Labor data, to identify employers of U.S. citizens, organizations with U.S. citizenship membership and education resources for U.S. citizens or dependents, to aid in targeting IRS education and compliance projects;

- identify local tax practitioners used by U.S. citizens and provide the practitioners with the resources and education necessary to improve compliance with U.S. tax laws;

- identify local media outlets accessed by U.S. citizens and develop specialized media releases to educate U.S. citizens regarding identified areas of non-compliance;

- develop and implement market segment education and compliance projects, similar to those described above;

- conduct compliance outreach and informational seminars; and

- initiate appropriate individual examinations and investigations.

These compliance-improvement methods are based in part on those used in IRS' successful Middle East Compliance Initiative, described above.

C. Factors Limiting Efforts to Measure and Improve Compliance

Several factors inhibit IRS efforts to measure and improve compliance levels. For example, there currently is limited detailed data regarding the number of U.S. citizens living overseas. *But see* Section II.A, *supra* (describing a demographic study that will provide estimates of tax filing and payment compliance rates). In addition, as discussed in Part III, *infra*, federal agencies such as the Department of State ("DOS") and the Social Security Administration historically have restricted IRS' access to agency data that might help IRS identify overseas Americans.[12]

Moreover, the IRS' Information Returns Program ("IRP"), which matches information from third-party payors (such as employers and financial institutions) with individual tax returns, and is one of IRS' primary enforcement tools, is of little help in identifying potential noncompliance by overseas taxpayers. Unless overseas individuals work for a U.S. employer, generally no easily usable wage or salary information will be reported to the IRS with respect to such individuals. This is because the IRP matching program generally does not receive third-party wage or salary information it can match to the returns of American independent contractors working overseas, of American employees of foreign corporations working overseas, or of American retired persons with income from foreign pensions. If such an individual no longer has investments in the United States, IRS may receive no

---

[12]It is the position of the DOS that the restriction on DOS data is required by the Privacy Act, 5 U.S.C. § 552a.

IRP documents at all with respect to the individual,[13] and thus IRS may not be able to determine whether or not such an individual should have filed a U.S. income tax return.

Other factors also operate to limit both compliance measurement and improvement. Because the United States asserts taxing jurisdiction over those with little or no connection to the United States other than citizenship or status as a lawful permanent resident, in many cases overseas U.S. taxpayers are difficult to trace or contact. Moreover, even when valid tax assessments can be made against overseas taxpayers, IRS has limited enforcement recourse if the taxpayer's assets are physically located outside of the United States.

In addition, persons may be unaware of their status as U.S. taxpayers with an obligation to file a U.S. tax return. As described in Section II.B, *supra*, IRS has undertaken various taxpayer education initiatives to increase awareness of filing and payment obligations. In some cases, however, education may not be sufficient. For example, an individual who was born outside the United States and has never even visited the country may, nevertheless, be a U.S. citizen by reason of his parents' U.S. citizenship. Such a person may not even know that he is a U.S. citizen and thus likely will not know of his obligation to file a U.S. tax return. Similarly, the United States imposes tax on green card holders who no longer reside in the United States but who have not surrendered their green cards. Although the immigration laws may no longer recognize the validity of the green card if the holder attempted to reenter the country, and the individual may no longer consider himself entitled to lawful permanent resident status, the individual remains subject to U.S. tax under the Code.

Thus, although U.S. citizenship and lawful permanent resident status are valued and valuable,

---

[13]Pursuant to regulations issued under Code section 1441, agreements are authorized with certain foreign financial institutions pursuant to which, beginning in the year 2000, the United States may receive information with respect to payments made by or through such institutions to U.S. persons.

and provide a sound basis for U.S. taxation of worldwide income, compliance enforcement by IRS may be extremely difficult with respect to individuals whose connection to this country was or will be minimal. In some limited cases, efficiency and equity may argue for some modification of the rules leading to such noncompliance. *See* Part IV, *infra*.

III. Sharing of Information Between Agencies

A. Information from Department of State Regarding U.S. Citizens and Former U.S. Citizens Living Abroad

1. Individuals Who Retain Citizenship

a. Passport Data (Code Section 6039E)

Code section 6039E, added by the Tax Reform Act of 1986, requires DOS to collect certain information from U.S. passport applicants and forward that information to IRS. The section provides that any individual who applies for a U.S. passport must provide: (i) the individual's taxpayer identification number (that is, the individual's Social Security number); (ii) any foreign country in which the individual is residing, and; (iii) any other information the Secretary of the Treasury may prescribe. Currently, DOS collects and sends to IRS each applicant's: (i) full name; (ii) Social Security number; (iii) mailing address; and (iv) date of birth. IRS processes through the IRP, discussed in Section II.C, *supra*, the information it receives from DOS to validate the Social Security number furnished by the applicant for use in the various IRP-based compliance programs. Individuals subject to potential civil penalties (*e.g.*, a passport applicant who fails to supply his Social Security number and is thereby liable for a $500 penalty under 6039E(c)) are also identified through this process.

15

IRS is currently considering whether obtaining additional information from DOS, such as each applicant's occupation, is worth the increased cost of obtaining such information. If it is determined that additional information should be required, the Secretary of the Treasury, pursuant to section 6039E(b)(4) of the Code, may prescribe that such information be provided by passport applicants; alternatively, such prescription may be made by agreement between IRS and DOS (and need not be made in regulations). Because IRS must pay DOS for each item of information transmitted to IRS, and in addition must pay to have DOS' computer systems reconfigured to collect such information to have DOS' personnel trained to collect and input such information and to have passport applications reprinted and redistributed, in addition to reconfiguring its own computer systems to process the additional information, IRS will weigh the potential benefit of obtaining such information against the cost.

Treasury and IRS have issued proposed regulations under section 6039E and are currently working towards finalizing those regulations. The regulations are being finalized primarily for reasons other than the collection of information on passport applications. For example, under 6039E(e), the Secretary of the Treasury is authorized to exempt any class of persons from the information provision requirements of section 6039E. Under the statute, such exemption must be made by regulations, unlike prescriptions by the Secretary that additional information be required on applications, which may under the statute be made by regulations, on the application itself or otherwise. The final regulations will continue to provide the Secretary of the Treasury with the flexibility granted in the statute to require that additional information be provided on passport applications without issuing regulations. Additional information will be required on passport applications and/or transmitted from DOS to IRS only after the determination is made that the benefit such information will provide outweighs its cost. It is not expected that the final regulations will set forth a definitive list of the information that must be collected from passport applicants, but instead will continue the existing practice of permitting IRS, in conjunction with State, to require collection and transmission only of those items of information that IRS determines justify the cost.

It should be noted that several factors limit the usefulness of the passport data collected by DOS in identifying U.S. citizens who reside overseas and in identifying who in that group may owe tax to the United States. For example, as cited in the 1993 GAO Report, the address listed on a passport application is not always a good indicator of whether the applicant currently lives overseas. Some persons who intend to move overseas apply for a passport when they are still U.S. residents with a U.S. address. Moreover, because passports are valid for 10 years, the address listed on the application may be out of date by the time the information becomes relevant for tax compliance purposes.

Another factor limiting the usefulness of the passport data is that the data is often incomplete. IRS frequently receives records from DOS with missing or erroneous Social Security numbers, because DOS is not required to verify the Social Security number that a passport applicant provides. Without a valid Social Security number, IRS cannot efficiently check whether the applicant has filed an income tax return. According to DOS, it would be difficult for DOS to delay or deny the issuance of a passport while awaiting Social Security number verification because the supplying of a Social Security number is not, and perhaps could not, be used by DOS in determining a person's eligibility for a U.S. passport.

Regarding the imposition of the $500 penalty for failing to supply required information, including a correct Social Security number, it should be noted that if a taxpayer fails to provide a valid

Social Security number, IRS' ability to locate the taxpayer and assess the penalty is limited. IRS can efficiently assess a penalty on an individual only after it has obtained a valid Social Security number for that individual from another source, which must be done manually with a substantial expenditure of time and resources. Furthermore, data from IRS and the U.S. Census Bureau that GAO has analyzed indicates that over 40% of passport applicants who did not provide a correct Social Security number on their passport application are under the age of 10 and that 65% are under the age of 20. Thus it may not be efficient, or even appropriate, for IRS, which is charged with administering the tax laws, to track down persons who may not in fact have a Social Security number and who in any case are likely to owe no tax. The IRS is currently considering whether it is a worthwhile allocation of resources to write to each passport applicant above a certain age who provides a foreign address but who did not provide a Social Security number on their passport application requesting that the applicant either provide a Social Security number or an explanation of why a Social Security number cannot be provided, and explaining to the applicant the consequences that can follow if a valid Social Security number is not provided.

Finally, and perhaps most importantly, once IRS has obtained a valid Social Security number for a passport applicant, either from DOS or through some other means, the number is often of limited usefulness in determining if a taxpayer identified as potentially living overseas owes United States taxes because, as discussed in Section II.C, above, IRS often has little or no third-party wage or other income information with respect to the taxpayer it can match to a return. Thus, even if IRS can determine that a return has not been filed with respect to a U.S. taxpayer living overseas, IRS should have more information either before it determines to commit resources for a further examination or before it even contacts the taxpayer, who may in fact not be required to file a return.

Such additional information, for example, past or present income and earnings, cannot reasonably be required on a passport application. As noted above, IRS is considering whether obtaining from DOS each applicant's occupation would profitably narrow the field of overseas non-filers enough to be worth the increased cost.

b.   Department of State Restrictions on Additional Information

Current law generally does not require the sharing of information between executive branch agencies with respect to individuals living abroad who retain their U.S. citizenship. As noted in Section II.C, *supra*, and in the 1993 GAO Report, DOS restricts IRS access to certain agency data that might help IRS identify overseas citizens. It is DOS' position, for example, that the Privacy Act, 5 U.S.C. § 552a, does not allow DOS to provide to IRS on a routine basis the names of citizens registered with U.S. consulates and embassies abroad. According to DOS, such a broad use of these records would be inconsistent with the purpose for which the information was collected, which is to protect U.S. citizens abroad.[14] As a result, DOS only provides to IRS "the current addresses of specifically identified taxpayers in connection with pending actions to collect taxes accrued, examinations, and/or other related tax activities." DOS Public Notice 2233, reprinted at 60 Fed. Reg. 39,469 (Aug. 2, 1995). That disclosure is consistent with the law enforcement exception to the Privacy Act, 5 U.S.C. § 552a.

The DOS policy was summarized in the 1993 GAO Report, which observed that:

the State Department has denied IRS requests for general access to its lists of Americans who

---

[14]To carry out that function, DOS encourages overseas U.S. citizens to register with the nearest U.S. embassy or consulate. It is the position of DOS that routine disclosure of registration information to the IRS would discourage citizens from registering.

register at U.S. embassies and consulates contending that disclosure would violate the Privacy Act [5 U.S.C. § 552a]. The content of State Department lists varies by post, but all lists include name, date, and place of birth of Americans who voluntarily register at these posts; lists include some local addresses as well. In addition to Privacy Act concerns, State is also concerned that disclosing this information to IRS would discourage persons from registering with the posts. The State Department encourages persons to register their whereabouts with the posts so it can carry out its mission to protect Americans while they are in foreign countries. [1993 GAO Report, p. 8].

DOS' concern about sharing information on overseas citizens is also reflected in its memorandum dated February 9, 1993, reprinted in the 1993 GAO Report, Appendix V, p. 27, which states:

. . . IRS should not be given the names and addresses of Amcits [American citizens] registered at overseas posts because the mission of OCS [Overseas Citizens Services] to encourage the registration of Amcits with posts could be adversely impacted if the Amcits were aware that data regarding their whereabouts would be reported to IRS. This human safety objective of OCS is paramount to the fiscal objectives of the IRS.

IRS believes that the receipt of information from DOS regarding U.S. citizens registered at overseas DOS posts might aid it in tracking tax compliance by citizens living abroad. However, the Privacy Act may constrain the release of this information and thus any change in the current policy of DOS regarding the exchange of this information might require legislative action.[15] In addition, for the information to be of use to IRS, it would need to include Social Security numbers, which, we understand, are not routinely provided or requested. We should note, however, that we recognize that requesting a Social Security number would raise legitimate privacy and other concerns.

---

[15]Even if this information were provided by DOS, IRS would still not have reliable information on U.S. citizens living overseas who do not register with a U.S. embassy or consulate. IRS recognizes that those engaging in the most egregious tax avoidance may be likely to fall within the class of those who do not register.

Moreover, it should also be noted that even if a Social Security number were obtained by DOS, to the extent the information provided to IRS included only name, address and Social Security number, its usefulness would be limited for the reasons discussed in Section III.A.1.a, *supra*, with respect to passport data.

2. Individuals Who Lose Citizenship (Code Section 6039G)

The Act added to the Code provisions that facilitate information sharing between DOS and IRS regarding expatriating U.S. citizens. *See* Act § 512.[16] Section 6039G of the Code requires any individual who loses U.S. citizenship to provide a statement to DOS containing certain information, which DOS forwards to IRS (along with the names and other identifying information of expatriating individuals who refuse to complete the statement). *See* Code §§ 6039G(a), (e)(1). The section provides that any individual who loses U.S. citizenship must provide: (i) the individual's taxpayer identification number (that is, the individual's Social Security number); (ii) the mailing address of the individual's principal foreign residence; (iii) the foreign country in which such individual is residing; (iv) the foreign country of which such individual is a citizen; (v) in certain cases, information detailing the individual's assets and liabilities, and; (vi) any other information the Secretary of the Treasury may prescribe. Code § 6039G(b). IRS has issued guidance to taxpayers regarding the information

---

[16]Section 512 of the Act purported to add the provisions as section 6039F of the Code. Section 1905 of the Small Business Job Protection Act of 1996, Pub. L. 104-188, which was enacted the day before the Act, also added to the Code a section numbered 6039F. By technical amendment, the provisions added by the Act were re-designated as Code section 6039G. *See* section 1602(h) of the Taxpayer Relief Act of 1997, Pub. L. 105-34.

statement required under section 6039G. *See* Notice 97-19, 1997-10 I.R.B. 40.[17] IRS, in cooperation with DOS, has established procedures by which the information submitted to DOS is forwarded to IRS.

In addition, Code section 6039G requires DOS to provide IRS with a copy of each certificate of loss of nationality ("CLN") that is approved by the Secretary of State.[18] *See* Code § 6039G(e)(2). IRS and DOS have established procedures by which the copies are forwarded to IRS. All CLNs are manually reviewed by IRS and the information contained therein is entered into an IRS database. IRS then publishes the names received from DOS, as required by section 6039G(e). *See* 62 Fed. Reg. 4570 (Jan. 30, 1997); 62 Fed. Reg. 23,532 (Apr. 30, 1997); 62 Fed. Reg. 39,305 (July 22, 1997); 62 Fed. Reg. 59,758 (Nov. 4, 1997); 63 Fed. Reg. 6606 (Feb. 9, 1998). IRS is currently establishing a process by which those individuals who do not provide the information required under section 6039G will receive a letter from IRS explaining the requirements and requesting the information. IRS will use the database created with the information received from DOS pursuant to section 6039G to monitor and ensure compliance with section 877 of the Code, discussed in Section I.C *supra*, pursuant to which certain expatriates may be subject to continued U.S. taxation for the ten-year period following their expatriating act.

It should be noted, however, that the CLN form currently utilized by DOS does not contain the expatriate's Social Security number. Without that number, it may be difficult for IRS to match

---

[17]This notice also provides detailed guidance regarding section 877 of the Code, as amended by the Act.

[18]Prior to the Act, DOS was concerned that it lacked statutory authority to routinely provide copies of CLNs to IRS. *See* DOS letter to the Joint Committee on Taxation ("JCT"), dated May 9, 1995 (reprinted in the JCT report entitled *Issues Presented by Proposals to Modify the Tax Treatment of Expatriation*, JCS-17-95, at G-56 (the "JCT Report")).

the CLNs it receives under section 6039G(e)(2) with other taxpayer data. We understand that DOS intends to revise the CLN form to include the expatriate's Social Security number. It should be noted, however, that, as discussed in Section IV.A, *infra*, the CLN may be approved years after the date U.S. citizenship is considered lost for tax and nationality law purposes, and thus the CLN copies provided to IRS may prove to be of limited usefulness in identifying currently non-complying expatriates, because the expatriate may be difficult to track so long after the expatriating act and because the ten-year period under Code section 877 during which the expatriate might be subject to U.S. tax may already have run.

B.   **Information from INS Regarding Lawful Permanent Residents Living Abroad**

1.   **Individuals Who Retain Green Card**

a.   **Green Card Data (Code Section 6039E)**

Section 6039E, in addition to requiring DOS to collect information from U.S. citizens who apply for a passport, as discussed in Section III.A.1.a, *supra*, requires the Immigration and Naturalization Service ("INS") to collect certain information from each non-U.S. citizen who applies for a green card and to forward that information to IRS. The section provides that any individual who applies to be lawfully accorded the privilege of residing permanently in the United States as an immigrant must provide: (i) the individual's taxpayer identification number (if any); (ii) information with respect to whether such individual was required to file an income tax return in the last three years, and; (iii) any other information the Secretary of the Treasury may prescribe.[19] IRS' Office of Assistant Commissioner (Collection) uses the information to determine whether there has been any

---

[19]The information is collected on IRS Form 9003.

23

past tax noncompliance by the applicant.

With respect to using the information to improve compliance by green card holders residing overseas, it should be noted that overseas residence may be incompatible with retention of a green card, which is premised in the individual's being a resident of the United States.[20] The class of green card holders residing overseas should therefore be limited, and thus any information with respect to that class may be of limited usefulness in any effort to improve overall U.S. tax compliance by persons residing overseas. Moreover, although section 6039E of the Code requires INS to collect the applicant's tax identification number, *see* Code § 6039E(b)(1), it is Treasury's understanding that many green card applicants do not yet have a Social Security number or other tax identification number at the time of their application. For reasons similar to those discussed in Section III.A.1.a, *supra*, to the extent that the information submitted under section 6039E(b)(1) does not include such a number, it is difficult for IRS to use the information for tax compliance purposes. It is likely not a worthwhile allocation of resources to write to each applicant who did not provide a number requesting that a number be provided, because, as just noted, it appears that many green card

---

[20]According to INS, were INS aware that a green card holder resided outside the United States, INS would examine that person's continuing eligibility for green card status. It is Treasury's understanding that some green card holders may have taken the position on their U.S. tax returns that they are entitled to benefits under a U.S. income tax treaty because they are residents under the treaty of the treaty partner country. Such a position may be inconsistent with the individual's status for immigration law purposes as a green card holder, which, according to INS, is premised on the individual's being a permanent resident of the United States (such a position is *not* inconsistent with U.S. tax law, *see* Treas. Reg. § 301.7701(b)-7(a) (discussing residency determinations for purposes of income tax treaties with respect to individuals who would otherwise be residents both of the U.S. and of a treaty partner). INS representatives have informed Treasury that they would like to be notified of any green card holder who takes such a position on a U.S. tax return so that the person's continuing eligibility for green card status can be examined. However, Code section 6103 (relating to the confidentiality and disclosure of tax return information) currently does not permit IRS to convey that information to INS.

applicants do not in fact have a Social Security number or other tax identification number when they apply for a green card.

b.   INS Databases

Based on discussions with INS representatives, it is Treasury's understanding that INS databases contain records for approximately 10.5 million individuals who have been issued green cards and whose status has not been revoked or administratively or judicially determined to have been abandoned. Several factors, however, limit the usefulness of the INS databases for purposes of increasing tax compliance among those green card holders who reside outside the United States. It is Treasury's understanding that INS records do not indicate whether a green card holder is outside the United States. As a result, it may not be feasible to use the INS data as the basis of a compliance initiative aimed at overseas taxpayers. In fact, were INS aware that a green card holder resided outside the United States, INS would examine that person's continuing eligibility for green card status, because, as noted above, such status is premised on the individual's being a permanent resident of the United States. Moreover, as noted in Section III.A.1.a, *supra*, with respect to passport data, to the extent the records do not contain Social Security numbers, it is not feasible for IRS to use the records in any large-scale tax compliance initiative.

Representatives of Treasury and IRS have been meeting with representatives of INS to improve information sharing between the two agencies. Although some concerns, discussed below, still exist, these meetings have been productive. For example, IRS informed INS of the importance for tax enforcement purposes of including Social Security numbers with data furnished to IRS. Because an individual's Social Security number has not traditionally been necessary for INS to carry

25

out its mission, the INS databases do not include these numbers for many green card holders. However, INS has informed IRS that as a result of the meetings, it is currently attempting to add Social Security number fields to its databases of green card holders.

2. Green Card Holders Whose Status is Revoked/Determined to Be Abandoned

The Act contains provisions intended to facilitate information sharing between IRS and INS with respect to certain lawful permanent residents. Section 6039G(e)(3) requires INS to provide IRS with the name of each lawful permanent resident of the United States whose status has been revoked or has been administratively or judicially determined to have been abandoned.[21]

IRS, in cooperation with INS, has established a procedure by which the information is submitted to IRS. IRS will conduct random sampling on a yearly basis with respect to this information and attempt to determine whether former lawful permanent residents have complied with their past U.S. tax obligations or continued U.S. tax obligations under section 877 of the Code as amended by the Act, discussed in Section I.C, *supra*.

Several factors may hamper the attempt, however. Section 6039G(e)(3) of the Code does not explicitly require INS, in providing information to IRS, to identify whether a green card holder

---

[21]The Act also requires each long-term resident (defined as a person who has been a lawful permanent resident for at least 8 of the last 15 years) who ceases to be taxed as a resident to file an information statement similar to that filed by expatriating U.S. citizens. Code § 6039G(f). Unlike an expatriating citizen, who files the statement with DOS, a former long-term lawful permanent resident does not provide his or her statement to an intermediary agency, such as the INS, but instead files it directly with IRS as an attachment to the individual's tax return for the taxable year in which the triggering event takes place. IRS has issued detailed guidance to taxpayers regarding the information statement required under section 6039G, and is currently developing a form to collect this information. *See* Notice 97-19, 1997-10 I.R.B. 40.

whose status is revoked or determined to have been abandoned meets the section 877(e)(2) definition of "long-term resident" (*i.e.*, a lawful permanent resident in 8 of the last 15 years). That is, the information currently provided by INS to IRS is not sufficient in itself for IRS to determine whether the former green card holder may be subject to continued U.S. taxation under section 877 of the Code as amended by the Act. Because loss of long-term resident status may make a former lawful permanent resident subject to continued U.S. tax, IRS and INS are currently discussing the feasibility of having INS include the dates of lawful permanent resident status with the list of names required to be provided by section 6039G(e)(3). IRS would use this information to enforce compliance by those former lawful permanent residents who are subject to continuing U.S. tax after the loss of their status as lawful permanent residents under Code section 877.

A further potential problem may exist regarding the practical usefulness of the information to be provided by INS under section 6039G(e)(3). As noted in Section III.B.2, *supra*, the INS computer databases of green card holders currently do not contain Social Security numbers for many of the individuals. Absent a Social Security number, it will be difficult to match the list of former lawful permanent residents provided by INS against IRS' taxpayer records. However, INS representatives have informed Treasury that INS is attempting to remedy this problem by adding Social Security number fields to its databases of green card holders.

IV.   Definition of Individuals Subject to U.S. Taxation

As discussed in Part I and Section II.C, *supra*, the United States asserts broad tax jurisdiction over its citizens and resident aliens (including green card holders). Each citizen and resident alien is subject to U.S. filing requirements and, in general, is taxable on worldwide income regardless of whether he or she resides in the United States or abroad.[22]

This broad application of U.S. taxing power to U.S. citizens is justified in part by the fact that citizens enjoy important benefits of citizenship even while residing abroad. *See Cook v. Tait*, 265 U.S. 47 (1924). For example, a U.S. citizen can travel on a U.S. passport and may utilize the protection of U.S. embassies or consulates while overseas. Similarly, worldwide taxation of lawful permanent residents is justified in part by the important benefits associated with green card status, such as the right to depart and re-enter the United States and to reside here permanently.

As discussed in more detail below, the current law's determination of when an individual ceases to be a U.S. citizen for tax purposes may allow certain expatriating citizens to avoid U.S. worldwide taxing jurisdiction for periods when they might have been entitled to receive the benefits of U.S. citizenship. In contrast, certain lawful permanent residents may be subjected to worldwide tax liability even though the primary benefit associated with their green cards -- the right to re-enter the United States -- may be no longer recognized by INS.

Modifying the definitions of citizen and lawful permanent resident for tax purposes as set forth in Sections IV.A.2 and IV.B, *infra*, might address those concerns and may be advisable not only as a matter of tax policy, but also from a tax administration standpoint, because it would enhance IRS' ability to focus its compliance resources on those individuals living overseas from whom collection of additional tax revenues might be more likely. In addition, with respect to "unknowing" and "restored" citizens, discussed in Section IV.A.2.b, *infra*, equity may argue for some limited compliance exceptions. It should be noted that the inclusion in the report of the possible changes to

---

[22]Certain provisions, such as the foreign earned income exclusion and the foreign tax credit, discussed above, as well as bilateral income tax treaties, may lower U.S. taxes owed and may mitigate the potential double taxation that may arise under this broad jurisdiction.

these definitions (like the inclusion of possible changes to the expatriation taxation rules in Section I.C, *supra*) is intended to serve as a basis for discussion, and not as a legislative recommendation.

A.   Definition of U.S. Citizen for Tax Purposes

Under current law, an individual's status as a citizen for tax purposes, including when such status is lost, is governed by the relevant provisions of the Immigration and Nationality Act, 8 U.S.C. § 1401 *et seq.*[23] Treas. Reg. § 1.1-1(c). Historically, an individual lost U.S. citizenship when he or she committed one of several acts specified in the nationality laws (*e.g.*, voting in a foreign election or marrying a national of another country (the latter applied only to women)), regardless of the individual's motive in committing the act. *See* INA § 349 [8 U.S.C. § 1481 (1982)].

However, in 1967, the U.S. Supreme Court ruled that an individual may not be stripped of U.S. citizenship merely because he or she commits a certain act. An individual may lose citizenship only if the specified act was committed voluntarily and with the intention of renouncing U.S. citizenship. *Afroyim v. Rusk*, 387 U.S. 253 (1967). As a result, in 1986, Congress amended the INA to state expressly that an individual will not lose his or her citizenship by performing a listed act unless the act was voluntarily performed with the intention of relinquishing U.S. citizenship. INA § 349 [8 U.S.C. § 1481(a) (1986)].

The acts that result in loss of citizenship when performed voluntarily and with the requisite intent fall into two general categories. First, a U.S. citizen can formally renounce citizenship pursuant to section 349(a)(5) of the INA. This requires executing an oath of renunciation before a U.S.

---

[23]However, section 877, as revised by the Act, provides that an individual's loss of U.S. citizenship is fully recognized for tax purposes only if that the loss did not have for one of its principal purposes the avoidance of U.S. tax.

consular or diplomatic officer outside the United States in the form prescribed by the Secretary of State.[24] The individual's loss of citizenship is effective on the date the oath of renunciation is executed before the officer overseas.

Second, a citizen can voluntarily perform with the requisite intent one of the potentially expatriating acts listed in section 349(a) of the INA.[25] Briefly stated, these acts include:

(1)   obtaining naturalization in a foreign state;

(2)   taking an oath, affirmation or other formal declaration of allegiance to a foreign state;

(3)   entering or serving in the armed forces of a foreign state engaged in hostilities against the United States, or serving as a commissioned or non-commissioned officer in the armed forces of a foreign state; and

(4)   accepting employment with a foreign government if the individual has the nationality of that foreign state or a declaration of allegiance is required in accepting the position.

In cases involving one of these potentially expatriating acts, any loss of citizenship is considered effective on the date the act is committed, even though the loss may not be documented by DOS until a later date. DOS generally learns of a case of possible loss of citizenship arising from one of these acts only when the individual appears before a consular officer and acknowledges that the potentially expatriating act was committed voluntarily and with the requisite intent.[26]

---

[24]A citizen can also make a formal written renunciation of U.S. citizenship *within* the United States, but only in time of war. INA § 349(a)(6).

[25]One other act -- conviction for an act of treason -- can cause an individual to lose U.S. citizenship. INA § 349(a)(7). According to DOS representatives, this provision has not, in fact, been used to revoke an individual's citizenship.

[26]In both formal renunciation cases and losses of citizenship based on one of the above acts, INA § 358 requires the consular officer abroad to submit for approval a CLN to DOS. The date on which the CLN is approved, ordinarily two weeks to six months after submission, is *not* the effective date for loss of citizenship.

Under the foregoing procedures, two factual issues are of primary relevance: the date a potentially expatriating act under INA sections 349(a)(1)-(4) occurred; and whether at the time the act was committed the individual had the intent to relinquish U.S. citizenship in committing the act. With respect to the first issue, it is Treasury's understanding that the consular officer before whom an individual appears generally does not question the occurrence of the potentially expatriating act, or its alleged date, if the individual provides supporting documentation from a foreign government. So long as the consular officer is provided with such documentation, then, according to DOS, the consular officer has little or no grounds to question when or whether the act actually occurred.

With respect to the second issue, DOS policy sets forth the procedure by which DOS determines whether a potentially expatriating act was performed with the requisite intent. This official policy states:

> The Department has a uniform administrative standard of evidence based on the premise that U.S. citizens intend to retain United States citizenship when they obtain naturalization in a foreign state, subscribe to routine declarations of allegiance to a foreign state, or accept non-policy level employment with a foreign government. . . .
>
> In light of the administrative premise discussed above, a person who:
> (1) is naturalized in a foreign country;
> (2) takes a routine oath of allegiance; or
> (3) accepts non-policy level employment with a foreign government
> and in so doing wishes to retain U.S. citizenship need not submit prior to the commission of a potentially expatriating act a statement or evidence of his or her intent to retain U.S. citizenship since such an intent will be presumed.
>
> When such cases come to the attention of a U.S. consular officer, the person concerned will be asked to complete a questionnaire to ascertain his or her intent toward U.S. citizenship. Unless the person affirmatively asserts in the questionnaire that it was his or her intention to relinquish U.S. citizenship, the consular officer will certify that it was *not* the person's intent to relinquish U.S. citizenship and,

consequently, find that the person has retained U.S. citizenship.[27]

As a result of this published DOS policy, an individual who commits a potentially expatriating act will be considered to retain his or her U.S. citizenship unless, and until, that individual contacts, or is contacted by, DOS and affirmatively asserts that the act was committed with an intent to expatriate. The policy does not limit the period of time during which an individual may notify DOS that a previously committed potentially expatriating act was performed with the intent to relinquish citizenship. Once the individual does notify DOS that a previously committed act was performed with the requisite intent, the date of citizenship loss is retroactive to the date the underlying act was committed. It is DOS' position that 8 U.S.C. § 1488, which states that U.S. citizenship is lost solely by the performance of certain acts or the fulfillment of certain conditions, compels the conclusion that loss of citizenship occurs upon the date of such performance or fulfillment.

It is Treasury's understanding that the consular officer does not ordinarily challenge an individual's declaration that a previously committed potentially expatriating act was performed with the intent to expatriate, because in the usual case the officer would have no information that would indicate a challenge is appropriate. It is the opinion of DOS that a declaration can be challenged only if the official is aware that the individual had sought the benefits of U.S. citizenship (*e.g.*, applied for a passport) or had provided inconsistent public statements after the commission of the potentially expatriating act. DOS believes that this deference to the individual's assertion is required by the

---

[27]The DOS official policy is attached as Tab 2 to the DOS letter to JCT, dated May 9, 1995, reprinted in JCT Report at G-59. The DOS policy states one exception to this general rule. If an individual "[performs] an act made potentially expatriating by statute accompanied by conduct which is so inconsistent with retention of U.S. citizenship that it compels a conclusion that the individual intended to relinquish U.S. citizenship," DOS may consider the individual to have relinquished U.S. citizenship even if the individual does not contact a consular officer to declare his or her intention. According to the DOS administrative release, "such cases are very rare". *See* JCT Report at G-59.

Supreme Court decisions in *Afroyim v. Rusk*, 387 U.S. 253 (1967), and *Vance v. Terrazas*, 444 U.S. 252 (1980), which hold that a loss of citizenship requires specific subjective intent based on the individual's words or a fair inference from his or her proved conduct.

Under these DOS rules, an individual who is considering expatriating has wide latitude in controlling whether his or her loss of citizenship is recognized by DOS and the date on which the loss is effective. In the context of taxation, this latitude provides a potential expatriate with the ability to engage in significant tax planning.

For example, an individual who is considering expatriating for tax purposes may, as the first step in the process, obtain naturalization in another state.[28] As explained above, the mere performance of this potentially expatriating act, without notification to DOS of the individual's intent to expatriate, would not cause the individual to lose his U.S. citizenship. The individual could delay reporting his intent to a consular official, thereby retaining his ability to invoke his U.S. citizenship if, for example, an emergency arose and he needed the assistance of a U.S. embassy or consulate. If no such need arose, the individual could wait until some future time to notify a U.S. consular official of his prior potentially expatriating act. Absent evidence of travel on a U.S. passport or of any other acts unequivocally indicating that the person had held himself out as a U.S. citizen, the consular officer would accept without challenge the individual's declaration that he intended to relinquish his U.S. citizenship at the time of the earlier act. It is the position of DOS that absent such

---

[28]Indeed, a well-known book advising potential expatriates advises: "If there is any possibility that you might want to become a tax exile from the US at any time in the future you should get another nationality and a second passport now." Langer, The Tax Exile Report (2d ed. 1993-1994), at 67.

evidence the consular officer would have little or no legal basis to challenge the declaration.[29]

Because any such loss of citizenship would be retroactive to the date of the potentially expatriating act, the individual may not be taxable as a U.S. citizen during the period between the date of the act and the date the individual notified DOS. That retroactivity allows the tax-motivated expatriate to determine after the fact whether an expatriation effective from the earlier date would be tax advantageous now. In addition, the running of the ten-year period of taxation under section 877 may be deemed to have started at the date of the potentially expatriating act and may in fact have fully run by the time the expatriate notifies DOS, thus preventing IRS from asserting a present (and future) tax liability pursuant to section 877. Furthermore, the statute of limitation with respect to the earlier years may have run, preventing IRS from examining those earlier years.

The DOS rules thus allow a result that appears inconsistent with the "benefit" rationale underlying the United States' jurisdiction to tax its citizens noted in Part IV, *supra*, because the individual may not be subject to tax as a citizen during a period when he would have been able to invoke the benefits of U.S. citizenship. Moreover, the rules may allow a possible mechanism for avoidance of U.S. taxation through expatriation that may still be available despite the Act's amendment of the expatriation provisions of the Code.

The potential problems just described with respect to the taxation of expatriates may be remedied by either: (i) a modification of the nationality law definition of when citizenship is lost to eliminate the retroactive effect of citizenship loss determinations (which would result in a modification

---

[29]That DOS position is again based on its reading of *Afroyim v. Rusk*, 387 U.S. 253 (1967), and *Vance v. Terrazas*, 444 U.S. 252 (1980), which look to an individual's specific subjective intent. DOS believes that it is unlikely that in a given case a consular officer would possess information that could successfully impeach a person's assertion as to such person's state of mind.

of the tax law definition of when citizenship is lost); or (ii) a modification simply of the tax law definition of when citizenship is lost to eliminate the retroactive effect for tax purposes of DOS citizenship loss determinations.

1.   Modification of Nationality Law Definition

In 1995, the Administration proposed the DOS-initiated Consular Efficiency Act of 1995. Among other provisions, that proposed law would have eliminated the list of potentially expatriating acts under existing nationality law that can result in the loss of U.S. citizenship. Instead, the proposed law would provide that the only way that an individual could lose U.S. citizenship would be to take an oath of renunciation before a U.S. consular official. Moreover, the loss of citizenship would not be effective until the date such an oath was taken.

Under the proposed legislation, DOS would no longer have had to determine whether a potentially expatriating act may have occurred years earlier. For example, under the proposal, an individual who became a foreign national would continue to be a U.S. citizen for nationality law purposes until he or she renounced citizenship before a U.S. consular official, even if he or she became a foreign national with the contemporaneous intent of renouncing U.S. citizenship. Because the current tax law definition of citizenship follows the nationality law definition, the modification to the nationality law would prevent a potential expatriate from utilizing the significant tax planning described in Section IV.A, *supra*. The potential expatriate would no longer be able to have his loss of citizenship recognized retroactively and thereby possibly avoid U.S. tax liability premised on citizenship or based on former citizenship under section 877 of the Code for period after the performance of the potentially expatriating act and before notification of DOS of the prior performance of the act with the requisite intent. *See* Section IV.A, *supra*.

DOS is currently considering whether to re-submit the proposal, in the form just described or in a modified form.

2. Modification of Tax Law Definition

a. Elimination of Retroactive Effect of Citizenship Loss

As an alternative to amending the nationality law definition of when citizenship is lost, the tax law could be modified to provide that, for purposes of determining whether a person is taxed as a U.S. citizen, a DOS determination of citizenship loss shall not be given retroactive effect. Instead, an individual would be deemed to lose U.S. citizenship for tax purposes at the time the individual swears to a consular official that he or she intended to lose citizenship.

This modification would be consistent with the "benefits" rationale underlying the United States taxation of its citizens, and would prevent the potential manipulation described in Section IV.A, *supra*. An individual could no longer obtain naturalization in another country as a means of tax planning, only to delay notifying DOS of an intent to expatriate until some future time. Under the modification, such an individual would be subject to tax as a U.S. citizen until DOS was notified of the individual's potentially expatriating act and the requisite intent to expatriate. In effect, the modification would provide that an individual's citizenship status for tax purposes comport with DOS' contemporaneous view of the individual's status: The individual would be taxed as a U.S. citizen during those periods when, if contemporaneously asked, DOS would have considered the person to be a U.S. citizen based on the information it had at that time.

This modification would also remove the possible tax incentive to fabricate the date of a potentially expatriating act. For example, if an individual could obtain naturalization documents that were backdated, then the date on the document likely would be the date recorded on the CLN as the date citizenship was lost.[30] By modifying the definition of citizenship for tax purposes as discussed, the purported date of the foreign naturalization papers would be irrelevant for purposes of determining U.S. tax status.[31]

There are sound theoretical bases for the definitional modification. The definitional modification would result in persons being subject to U.S. tax during those periods DOS would have contemporaneously considered the person to be a U.S. citizen. The proposition that a person should *not* be subject to U.S. tax during those periods DOS would *not* have contemporaneously considered the person to be a U.S. citizen, has judicial support, even in those cases in which DOS later reinstated citizenship status retroactively. For example, in *United States v. D'Hotelle de Benitez Rexach*, 558 F.2d 37 (1st Cir. 1977), an individual committed an expatriating act in 1949, but did not act as a noncitizen until 1952, when DOS issued a CLN that retroactively revoked her U.S. citizenship. In 1965, as a result of a Supreme Court case invalidating a statute similar to that upon which the individual's expatriation had been based, DOS notified the taxpayer that her expatriation was void

---

[30]A U.S. consular officer would investigate if his suspicions were aroused that such practices had occurred.

[31]It should be noted that the proposed divergence of the tax law definition of citizenship from the nationality law definition of citizenship has some precedent in current law. For example, section 511(g)(3)(A) of the Act contains a transition provision for individuals who committed a potentially expatriating act prior to February 6, 1995 (the general effective date of the revised expatriation provisions) but who did not notify DOS of the act and intent to expatriate until after that date. Under the transition provision, section 877 as amended generally applies to such individuals even though their date of citizenship loss for purposes of the immigration law is retroactive to the date of the potentially expatriating act. Moreover, certain tax consequences of section 877(a) depend on the date that the individual notified DOS of the previously committed expatriating act, rather than the date of the potentially expatriating act.

and that DOS considered her a citizen. The court, in deciding the years for which the individual should be liable for U.S. taxes, focused on DOS' contemporaneous view of her citizenship status and the resulting benefits available to her during each period. Accordingly, the court ruled that from 1949 until 1952, during which DOS had not informed her of her loss of citizenship, the individual was subject to U.S. taxation. The court reasoned that, during that period, she was "privileged to travel on a United States passport; she received the protection of its government." *Id.* However, the court ruled that she should not be subject to U.S. taxation during the period from 1952 to 1965, because during that period DOS had treated her as a noncitizen. According to the court, the individual "cannot be dunned for taxes to support the United States government during the years in which she was denied its protection." *Id.*[32] The definitional modification simply would assure that a person could be dunned for taxes to support the United States government only during the years the DOS would have considered the person eligible for U.S. government protection.

b. Relief for "Unknowing" or "Restored" Citizens

An "unknowing" citizen is a person who genuinely does not know he or she is a U.S. citizen, and therefore does not avail himself or herself of the benefits of citizenship. The class of such persons

---

[32]See also Revenue Ruling 92-109, 1992-2 C.B. 3, which discusses several different fact situations regarding the retroactive reinstatement of citizenship, and bases each individual's tax status for a given period on the contemporaneous understanding of DOS. For example, the ruling considers an individual who, without the intent to relinquish citizenship, committed an expatriating act in 1981 and was issued a CLN in that year. In 1989, the individual requested that DOS review her loss of citizenship, and in 1990 DOS vacated her CLN and retroactively restored her U.S. citizenship. Despite the retroactivity of the DOS determination for nationality law purposes, the ruling holds that the individual was not liable for Federal income taxes as a citizen for 1981 through 1989. This ruling is consistent with that during the period from 1981 through 1989, DOS would not have contemporaneously recognized the individual's U.S. citizenship status.

could include, for example, individuals born outside the United States who were not aware of the identity, much less the U.S. citizenship status, of a biological parent.[33] Although it is impossible to measure the number of unknowing citizens living abroad, it may be significant. IRS has received numerous inquiries from executors of foreign estates who have concluded that the decedent technically was a U.S. citizen but did not know it.

Equity may argue for granting some unknowing and restored U.S. citizens an exemption from U.S. taxation. An individual claiming the benefit of this exemption should bear the burden of proving that he or she had no knowledge of his or her U.S. citizenship during the period at issue.[34] Because of the possibility of abuse, the criteria for lacking knowledge of U.S. citizenship should be strictly construed. Relevant factors may include:

(i)   absence of past statements to the U.S. government claiming citizenship (*e.g.*, passport

---

[33]In general, an individual born outside the United States to parents both of whom are U.S. citizens and at least one of whom has had a residence in the United States is a U.S. citizen. 8 U.S.C. § 1401(c). An individual born outside the United States on or after November 14, 1986 to one U.S. citizen parent and one non-citizen parent is a U.S. citizen if the citizen-parent was physically present in the United States for periods totaling at least five years, at least two of which were after attaining the age of 14. 8 U.S.C. § 1401(g). With respect to individuals born prior to November 14, 1986, to one U.S. citizen parent, the physical presence test for the citizen-parent is ten years with at least five being after attaining the age of 14. An individual born in the United States and subject to the jurisdiction thereof is a United States citizen, regardless of the nationality or residency of his parents. 8 U.S.C. § 1401(a); *see United States v. Wong Kim Ark*, 169 U.S. 649 (1898) (holding that a child of diplomats of a foreign state born in the United States was not a U.S. citizen because the child was not subject to the jurisdiction of the United States).

[34]Making use of a person's knowledge of his or her citizenship status is not unprecedented: DOS has previously applied the concept of unawareness of U.S. citizenship in administering the U.S. nationality laws. Prior to 1978, section 301(b) of the INA provided, in general, that a person born outside the United States to one U.S. citizen parent was required to live in the United States for two years between the ages of 14 and 28 in order to retain U.S. citizenship. If a person failed to meet this requirement but proved to DOS that he or she was unaware of a potential claim to U.S. citizenship, the person was held to have constructively complied with section 301(b) of the INA and was allowed to retain U.S. citizenship.

applications and filings for government benefits as a citizen); and

(ii)   past statements indicating a belief that he or she is not a U.S. citizen (*e.g.*, applications for employment, applications to educational institutions, financial transaction documentation, foreign tax returns, requests for a visa for travel to the United States, and entering the United States on a foreign passport).

Once an individual becomes aware of his or her U.S. citizenship or, based on objective facts, should have become aware of such status, the individual could under this regime have a period of time (*e.g.*, six months) to abandon that status without U.S. tax consequences (including the effects of section 877), so long as he or she does not utilize the benefits of citizenship during that period. *Cf.* 8 U.S.C. § 1483(b) (a U.S. citizen who commits a potentially expatriating act prior to his or her eighteenth birthday is not deemed to have lost citizenship if he or she asserts a claim to U.S. citizenship within six months after attaining the age of eighteen).

Similar criteria could be applied to grant "restored" citizens an exemption. A restored U.S. citizen is an individual who was treated by DOS as having lost U.S. citizenship under certain statutory provisions that were subsequently held to be unconstitutional by the Supreme Court, as discussed above. *See Afroyim v. Rusk*, 387 U.S. 253 (1967); *Schneider v. Rusk*, 377 U.S. 163 (1964). The term also includes an individual who was treated by DOS as having lost U.S. citizenship on the basis of an evidentiary standard of intent that was held impermissible by the Supreme Court. *See Vance v. Terrazas*, 444 U.S. 252 (1980) (the United States must prove that an individual had specific subjective intent to relinquish citizenship). In general, these cases, as well as lower court cases addressing the issue, retroactively restore U.S. citizenship to affected individuals (including children born to these individuals that would have been citizens by reason of the citizenship of the parent with restored citizenship). In so doing, the courts apparently assume that all affected individuals prefer to be U.S. citizens, without considering the adverse tax consequences that may result from the reinstatement of citizenship status. DOS estimates that several thousand individuals may be restored citizens who have not yet applied to DOS to have their CLNs vacated.

As discussed in Section IV.A.1.a, *supra*, IRS and the judiciary have attempted to provide relief from retroactive taxation for restored citizens for those periods when the individual's citizenship was not contemporaneously recognized by DOS. *See United States v. D'Hotelle de Benitez Rexach*, 558 F.2d 37 (1st Cir. 1977); Revenue Ruling 92-109, 1992-2 C.B. 3; *see also* Revenue Ruling 75-357, 1975-2 C.B. 5; Revenue Ruling 70-506, 1970-2 C.B. 1. However, the guidance and cases do not provide reliable relief for any citizens whose citizenship is restored after the issuance of the guidance or the judicial opinions, even for those persons who genuinely thought that they had ceased to be U.S. citizens and who have conducted their lives accordingly. For example, Revenue Ruling 92-109 states that an individual who applies after 1992 to DOS to have his or her CLN administratively reviewed and whose CLN is vacated (and whose citizenship is thus restored retroactively) is entitled to retroactive tax relief only for pre-1993 taxable years. Furthermore, if an individual expatriates upon learning of his restored U.S. citizenship status, he or she could be subject to tax under section 877.

The extent of the relief granted by the just-cited revenue rulings is based on Code section 7805(b)(8), which allows IRS to prescribe the extent to which a ruling shall be applied without retroactive effect. The rulings state the longstanding general rule that during any period a person is in fact a U.S. citizen for nationality law purposes that person is subject to U.S. taxation as a U.S. citizen, regardless of whether the person knows he is a citizen or whether the DOS would contemporaneously regard him as a citizen. The rulings then provide, however, that with respect to

41

the specific factual patterns being addressed, the general rule will be applied prospectively only, pursuant to IRS' authority under section 7805(b)(8) of the Code to limit the retroactive effect of rulings. Because the connection between the nationality law definition of citizenship and the tax law definition is both clear and longstanding and in light of the inherent limitations of providing prospective relief in this situation through administrative rulings, it is Treasury's view that further relief, if any, for restored citizens be effected by explicit statutory amendment. Specifically, the Code could be amended to provide that an individual who (i) committed an expatriating act under a provision that a court later held to be unconstitutional, and (ii) has not availed himself or herself of any benefit of U.S. citizenship since the occurrence of that act, will not be taxed as a citizen unless and until the individual applies to DOS to have his or her CLN administratively vacated or otherwise seeks to take advantage of the benefits of citizenship. In effect, such an amendment would allow individuals who genuinely thought that they had ceased to be U.S. citizens to decide whether to accept the benefits and burdens arising from the availability of restored citizenship. There may be other potential solutions that should be considered. Treasury is putting this idea forward as one possible solution to the problem identified.

B.   Definition of Lawful Permanent Resident Subject to Tax

An alien who obtains an immigrant visa is allowed to enter the United States with the intention of remaining permanently. These aliens are issued alien registration receipt cards, commonly referred to as "green cards". As noted above, these individuals are considered "lawful permanent residents" for tax purposes, and generally are taxed in the same manner as U.S. citizens. Code § 7701(b)(6).

Green card holders are allowed to leave the United States for temporary periods. Upon each re-entry, they are questioned by an INS representative as to their residency status. In general, a green card holder may remain outside the United States for up to 12 months without jeopardizing the validity of his or her green card.[35] However, an individual may remain outside the United States for up to 2 years if he or she obtained a re-entry permit prior to departing the United States. *See* INS letter to the Joint Committee on Taxation, dated May 31, 1995, reprinted in JCT Report at G-109.

If a green card holder remains outside the United States longer than permitted, he or she is provided the opportunity for a hearing before an immigration judge, who determines the alien's admissibility. If the individual is found excludable, his or her green card status is rescinded and the individual is not allowed to enter the United States. Similarly, a permanent resident who is deported from the United States has his or her green card canceled.

Code section 7701(b)(6) provides that a green card holder will no longer be considered a lawful permanent resident (and, therefore, no longer subject to U.S. worldwide taxation) if his or her status as such has been revoked or has been administratively or judicially determined to have been abandoned. For example, if a green card holder attempts to enter the United States after having remained outside the United States for longer than the permitted time discussed above, and if the individual is found excludable by the immigration judge, the individual will lose his green card status and will no longer be subject to taxation as a resident alien. Also, if an individual leaves the United States and does not intend to return, he or she may surrender the green card and will not be taxed as

---

[35]It is our understanding that many green card holders take advantage of the 12-month period described above by residing outside the United States for most of the year and returning to the United States once a year for the sole purpose of keeping their green cards valid. This practice appears inconsistent with the status of being a permanent resident of the United States inherent in the issuance of a green card. To the extent that this is a problem, it may be best remedied through a modification of the immigration laws. In the meantime, to the extent that individuals continue to receive the benefits of green card status through this practice, they should continue to be taxed as U.S. residents.

a resident alien in the future, unless he or she meets another test for resident alien status.[36]

If, however, a green card holder remains outside the United States for longer than the permitted period but does not attempt to re-enter the United States, no administrative or judicial proceeding will be undertaken regarding the validity of his or her green card. Accordingly, the individual will technically remain subject to worldwide U.S. tax jurisdiction under current law, even though his or her green card might no longer be recognized as valid by INS or an immigration judge.

The Code and immigration laws could be harmonized so that the U.S. no longer exercises worldwide tax jurisdiction over individuals to the extent the immigration laws would no longer hold the green card to be valid if the individual attempted to use it for re-entry, and the individual is able to document that fact. As noted above, worldwide taxation of green card holders is premised in part on the benefits available to such individuals. However, in the case of green card holders whose status as such would not be recognized as valid, the primary benefit associated with the status -- the ability to re-enter the United States -- is no longer present.[37]

V.   Conclusion and Recommendation

Because the United States taxes its citizens on their worldwide income, regardless of where they live, the United States has the responsibility of administering its tax laws with respect to persons who do not reside within the United States. Such persons are more likely to receive income from

---

[36]However, certain long-term green card holders may remain subject to tax under Code section 877, as amended by the Act.

[37]Were this approach to be adopted, some technical issues would need to be addressed, including, for example, how to take account of the fact that a green card might no longer be recognized as valid for re-entry by INS but its holder might successfully appeal to an immigration judge not to be excluded.

third-party payors, such as foreign employers and foreign financial institutions operating wholly outside the United States, that generally are not required to report to the United States the payment of income. Moreover, such overseas Americans are more likely to have assets beyond the reach of the United States government. These factors of physical distance, lack of third-party information returns and remote asset location combine to make the task of ensuring the compliance of overseas U.S. taxpayers with U.S. tax laws a challenge. Moreover, as discussed in Section I.B, *supra*, sections 901 and 911 of the Code operate in many instances to reduce or eliminate the U.S. tax that otherwise would be due from those non-filing overseas U.S. taxpayers that IRS is able to identify and contact.

The Internal Revenue Service has already responded to the challenge of improving compliance by overseas U.S. taxpayers. *See* Section II.B, *supra*. IRS intends to search for new ways to further improve compliance. Upon completion of its demographic study, discussed in Section II.A, *supra*, profiling on an aggregate, country-by-country basis the tax filing and payment compliance of U.S. citizens residing overseas, IRS will be positioned to focus its limited compliance resources on those countries and areas in which those resources will have the greatest effect. A draft of the report is scheduled for release later this summer. It is Treasury's belief that IRS' current compliance-improvement methods are fundamentally sound, and, as the experience of IRS' Middle East Initiative and other successful compliance initiatives shows, as discussed in Section II.B, *supra*, those methods can be both effective and cost-effective, when appropriately directed. Again, IRS' demographic study will help provide that direction.

IRS should focus its overseas compliance resources on compliance measurement and enforcement projects that are likely to yield sufficient tangible results to warrant the resource expenditure. For example, an overseas compliance initiative that is targeted based only upon the information available from passport applications may not be sufficiently successful. As discussed in Section III.A.1.a, *supra*, with only a list of passport applicants' names, dates of birth, mailing addresses and Social Security numbers, the IRS may not be able to determine where its overseas compliance resources can be best allocated and its compliance initiatives best be directed. Requiring that occupation be provided on passport applications for transmittal to IRS may not in and of itself provide IRS with sufficient additional information to allow IRS to make those determinations, and such information can be obtained only at significant cost to IRS. After completion of its demographic study, IRS will be better positioned to determine where its resources to improve overseas compliance should be directed.

It is therefore Treasury's recommendation that upon the completion of the IRS demographic study, IRS appropriately allocate its resources to projects and initiatives that properly balance the goal of efficient revenue collection with the legitimate privacy and other interests of Americans living and traveling overseas. Based on IRS' experience in its Middle East Compliance Initiative and other successful compliance initiatives, such efforts should include: analysis of local information sources, such as local financial news media and DOS and Department of Labor data, to identify employers of U.S. citizens, organizations with U.S. citizenship membership and education resources used by U.S. citizens or dependents, to aid in targeting education and compliance projects; identification of local tax practitioners used by U.S. citizens to provide such practitioners with the resources and education necessary to improve compliance with U.S. tax laws; identification of local media outlets accessed by U.S. citizens and development of specialized media releases to educate U.S. citizens regarding identified areas of non-compliance; development and implementation of market segment education and compliance projects; conducting outreach and informational seminars; and pursuing appropriate

46

individual examinations and investigations. IRS should continue and expand upon its recent, successful initiatives described in Section II.B, *supra*, to further improve compliance.

Consideration should also be given to modifying the basis for U.S. taxation of individuals. As discussed in Part IV, *supra*, the current definition of individuals subject to U.S. taxation may be subject to manipulation by tax-motivated expatriates, on the one hand, and may, on the other hand, include some individuals who for reasons of administrative efficiency and fundamental fairness should be excluded.

With respect to improving compliance through improved coordination between executive branch agencies, Treasury notes that although some executive agencies, such as DOS, may have information that might aid IRS in improving compliance (as discussed in Section III.A.1.b, *supra*), Treasury is cognizant of the fact that Privacy Act and other concerns may limit such agencies' ability to share such information with IRS. Treasury is also aware that to the extent other agencies do not organize their data by Social Security number, such data may be of limited usefulness to IRS in improving overseas compliance. Moreover, even if such data were organized by Social Security number, it may still be of limited usefulness to IRS, as discussed Sections III.A.1.a and III.B, *supra*. Treasury and IRS will continue to meet and coordinate with other executive agencies, such as has been done with INS, to improve information sharing and to improve the quality and usefulness of the information shared, always mindful, however, of the privacy law constraints under which each agency operates and the privacy concerns of the citizens the agencies serve. Treasury and IRS will also continue discussions with DOS regarding the feasibility, efficacy and costs of collecting additional information from passport applicants for use in improving tax filing and payment compliance by U.S. taxpayers residing overseas.

47

The material in this special afterword has been added by the publisher and is excerpted from several recently published books (available from bookstores and online booksellers) including:

- *Swiss Bank Accounts and Investment Management: Your Own Completely-Legal, Super-Safe, Tax-Free Offshore Account -- And Not Even The IRS Has To Know* by SwissInvesting.com
- *The Complete Guide to Tax Havens* by Adam Starchild
- *The Conservative Wealthbuilder* by Adam Starchild

Capital Preservation Through Global Investing

Investing globally is one of the most successful ways to accomplish capital preservation and growth. In books such as *The Complete Guide to Tax Havens* and *The Conservative Wealthbuilder: Capital Preservation Through Global Investing*, Adam Starchild reveals how you can create an ultimate global portfolio of investments to hedge against inflation, taxes, confiscations, market, fluctuations, currency devaluations, economic and political turmoil.

Starchild reveals the little-known investment secrets that he has been giving to his clients for the past few decades. His recommendations are not high-flying investment tips, but rather solid, conservative recommendations that over time will help build a healthy nest-egg for you.

You will learn how to build a secret stash of cash that:
- You can access at any time
- Is tax-free and seizure proof
- Pays competitive dividends and interest
- And has no government reporting requirements (even for Americans)

In fact, if you had put $ 10,000 each year into this investment or the last twenty years you would have $590,697 today!

You will also discover:

- How to accumulate income tax-free

- Why offshore mutual funds should form a vital part of your global portfolio

- How to invest in gold, silver and platinum and the investor potential of these precious metals

- Why Switzerland should play an essential part in any global nest-egg strategy

- How and where to best form an offshore trust in order to provide tax and creditor protection for your investments

- How to invest tax-free in the United States

Everything you need to get yourself started on a global path to a secure fortune is in *The Conservative Wealthbuilder*. Starchild's techniques have been used by many of the world's wealthiest people for decades, including presidents, kings, Arab sheiks... And now for the first time they are available to you. They have been tested and proven over time. You will not find a safer, surer path to financial security than that mapped out for you in this unique work!

The Conservative Wealthbuilder is available through major bookstores and online booksellers. *The Complete Guide to Tax Havens* provides a wealth of information on forming offshore corporations and trusts.

Investing for the Offshore Entity

Investing for the offshore entity is just as important as creating the corporation or trust in the first place. Failure to invest the corpus and reinvest the income is one of the surest ways to squander the benefits that come from creation of an offshore corporation or trust. Astute choices in investment can lead to the realization of personal financial goals and, potentially, financial freedom. A problem often arises when one considers where to invest his money because there are so many options. Selecting the wrong ones can, at best, hinder the achievement of financial goals, and, at the worst, result in financial ruin. It is important to bear in mind that the investing is as important as the creation and structuring of the offshore entity.

Offshore Asset Protection and Tax Deferral with Portfolio Bonds

A relatively new and little-known strategy for the wealthier investor is the offshore portfolio bond (also known as the private portfolio bond, offshore insurance bond, and similar names). This investment device combines the banking and insurance: It is a professionally managed offshore account with the benefits of both a traditional offshore trust and an offshore insurance investment. For U.S. investors with large retirement accounts, the portfolio bond can be used with a rollover account so that the portfolio bond becomes part of the retirement account, opening up a number of additional opportunities. (The minimum investment in a portfolio bond is generally 250,000 Swiss francs.)

The portfolio bond can be considered as a simple holding structure, eliminating the need for complex holding companies and trusts, and without the reporting requirements those entities require. Usually the portfolio bond is domiciled in an offshore tax haven, through which the investor (or his/her selected bank or adviser) can direct the insurance company to invest in a wide range of investment vehicles such as shares, unit trusts, cash deposits, bonds etc.

The investor enters into a contract in his name with an offshore insurance company. The offshore portfolio bond is an insurance policy or an annuity policy, not a securities account or bank account, so it does not have to be reported as an offshore account. The value is precisely the amount invested and the money grows as it is managed. The investor can select one or several money managers - either banks or independent investment advisors.

There are the usual benefits of confidentiality, individual asset allocation and strategy. But there are also unique benefits to this form of investment.

For estate planning purposes, the portfolio bond allows distributions separate from the ordinary probated estate, and allows the designation of any beneficiary (although there may be restriction is the investor is domiciled in a country that has some compulsory provisions as to legal heirs. Upon death the insurance company will transfer the money to the beneficiaries within a few days after receipt of the death certificate. Because it is an insurance policy, no power of attorney, no last will and no certificate of inheritance are required. The beneficiaries get immediate access to the money and it will be paid out according to the original directions, such as a lump sum or annual payments.

Properly structured and established in the right jurisdictions, portfolio bonds enjoy legal protection from creditors and cannot be seized or be included in any bankruptcy proceeding. The asset protection comes from the insurance part of the portfolio bond.

In some jurisdictions the law is very strict and the protection rock solid. If properly structured, the money is protected even if there is a judgment or court order against you. This major advantage is of particular interest to professionals, or anyone who is exposed to possible lawsuits, malpractice cases, nervous creditors or vengeful ex-spouses.

In some jurisdictions an offshore portfolio bond is secret by law. In Liechtenstein, for example, there is an insurance secrecy law analogous to the banking secrecy law in Switzerland. No information is provided to any third party (natural person or legal entity).

Unlike many other offshore investments, portfolio bonds are, in some jurisdictions, completely free of local taxes. No taxes are due if purchased in offshore jurisdictions like Switzerland or Liechtenstein. As far as income, capital gains and estate tax are concerned, the law of the investor's tax domicile is decisive.

In various countries insurance policies enjoy substantial tax benefits if correctly structured. Portfolio bonds offer utmost flexibility and can be tailor-made to fit the legal requirements for tax benefits in the investor's country.

The underlying investments can be freely selected. The portfolio can contain any investment of the investor's choice as long as the value can be established (e.g. non listed stock, real estate and shares of the client's own company etc.).

The portfolio bond provides utmost liquidity. Money can be added and taken out with a few days notice. If the investor has chosen a tax privileged solution, domestic tax law might require the funds to remain within the portfolio bond for a certain period or up to a certain age. But even then it is always possible to borrow against the portfolio bond.

The portfolio bond is a complex area of investment and tax planning, and it is important to work with an expert. A recommended contact in this field is NMG International Financial Services, Ltd., a subsidiary of The NMG Group, which was originally formed as an actuarial consulting and related financial services company in Singapore in 1991. Today, NMG has become the largest provider of financial services consulting in Asia, and has established itself as a market leader in specialist advice on emerging economies. NMG now has consulting operations and representation in 18 cities on six continents.

NMG International Financial Services Ltd. is domiciled in Zurich, Switzerland. It is an independent investment consultancy firm established to satisfy the investment and financial protection needs of international clients. They do this by selecting outstanding Swiss and international insurance and banking products while offering exceptional advice and service.

In addition to portfolio bonds, they do provide access to Swiss fixed and variable annuities, life insurance, and related products.

Contact:

Marc Sola or Maria Amstad
NMG International Financial Services Ltd.
Suite 5
Goethestrasse 22
CH-8022 Zurich, Switzerland
Telephone: +41-1-266-2141
Fax: +41-1-266-2149   Please mark fax "Attention: Suite 5"

or complete their online inquiry form on the Internet at http://www.swissinvesting.com/nmg/

Swiss Portfolio Management Experts

While there are many excellent Swiss investment financial managers, one of particular note is the management firm of Weber Hartmann Vrijhof & Partners. Offering management services for the portfolios of both individuals and companies, the firm excels at providing personal attention to its clients. Weber Hartmann Vrijhof & Partners was established in 1992 by Hans Weber, Robert Vrijhof, and Adrian Hartmann. The three men have substantial experience in finance and investment. Weber managed Foreign Commerce Bank (FOCOBANK) in Switzerland for nearly 30 years as its president and CEO, Vrijhof was a former vice-president and head of FOCOBANK'S portfolio management group, and Hartmann was head of FOCOBANK'S North American subsidiary in Vancouver. Weber Hartmann Vrijhof & Partners offers specialized investment services designed to meet the individual needs of their clients.

The minimum opening portfolio to be managed by this firm is $250,000 or equivalent. The management team here normally recommends that a portion of the portfolio be invested in hard currencies other than the U.S. dollar including the Swiss franc, French franc, German mark, and Dutch guilder. Respected for their conservative approach to portfolio management, the partners assist clients with opening a custodial account at one of the major private Swiss banks, so that all client securities are held by the bank, not the investment manager.

A large percentage of their clients are based in the United States. One of their main goals has always been to get a certain portion of their clients' wealth out of the U.S. dollar and into European hard currencies such as Swiss francs, Deutschmarks, and Dutch guilders, and then build a portfolio with a mix of bonds and shares.

If you wish to learn more about the services the firm offers, contact them at:

Weber Hartmann Vrijhof & Partners, Ltd.
Attn: New Clients Department
Zurichstrasse 110B
CH-8134 Adilswil
Switzerland
Tel: +41 1 709-11-15
Fax: +41 1 709-11-13, please mark fax "Attn: New Clients Department"

or complete their online inquiry form on the Internet at http://www.cyberhaven.com/whvp/

Even though many investors recognize that Switzerland is a center of finance and investment, they do not realize the vast scope of the investment options offered by Swiss financial institutions and companies. Switzerland is a prime spot for investment for numerous reasons, most importantly for the strength of its currency, security of its financial system, and steady returns on investment.